BUT GOD

BUT GOD

The Story Of The Kings

Karl & Kaydene King

Xulon Press

Xulon Press
555 Winderley Pl, Suite 225
Maitland, FL 32751
407.339.4217
www.xulonpress.com

Unless otherwise indicated, Scripture quotations taken from the Amplified Bible (AMP). Copyright © 2015 by The Lockman Foundation. Used by permission. All rights reserved.

Scripture quotations taken from the Holy Bible, New International Version (NIV). Copyright © 1973, 1978, 1984, 2011 by Biblica, Inc.™. Used by permission. All rights reserved.

Paperback ISBN-13: 978-1-66288-520-4
Ebook ISBN-13: 978-1-66288-521-1

Table of Contents

Introduction

IS GOD STILL in control? Is He still reigning in His sovereignty? Has He stopped being God at any given moment? Absolutely not! What about the attacks that are unseen to the physical eye, but were manifested in the realm of the physical, including the dire ones? Had He missed them? Absolutely not!

We were newly wedded! We exchanged our covenantal vows in the year 2018, and we had many plans for the near future. There was nothing that was unattainable. Did I forget to declare what the apostle James said? *"If it is the Lord's will, we will live and do this or that"* (James 4:15b NIV). I believe that we were in the center of God's will and plans. Were they visions for His appointed time and not ours? We were not privileged to execute much of what we had planned. Oh, how I was in for a very unpleasant surprise. Before long, I almost became a widow.

In 2021, one of our plans was to start our family when the enemy tried to eradicate not only our plans of becoming parents, but to cut Karl (my husband's) life short. But God's plans cannot be thwarted or restrained, not by the devil or by anyone. Therefore, the plan of the enemy was made null and void, as God is not through with Karl, neither is He through with us as a couple or as ministry partners (which was one of our plans that we were looking forward to executing).

MIRACLES STILL HAPPEN!

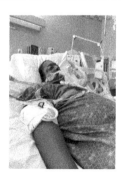

Introduction

In February of 2021, I would have been issued a death certificate for my husband, Karl. But God was not done with him yet. *"Then you will call on me and come and pray to me, and I will listen to you"* (Jer. 29:12 NIV). God listened and continues to listen to the cries of His saints! *"For the eyes of the Lord are [looking favorably] upon the righteous (the upright), and His ears are attentive to their prayer (eager to answer) …"* (1 Pet. 3:12 AMP).

We have prayed and believed in God for many things at various times, including for supernatural protection against the onslaught of the enemy, but we were not always spared the processes that have purposes attached to them. It was at those times that the preserving nature of God was revealed, and His covenant names were experienced.

The intended purpose of penning this book is to help others understand that the plans of God are always for good and not of evil (Jer. 29:11), even when it is birthed through evil and trying circumstances. God never wastes anything (Rom. 8:28), even the dire ones.

He turns pain into purpose. In the midst of every circumstance, He is always upholding us in the righteousness of His right hand (Isa. 41:10). This is indeed comforting!

There will be times when circumstances appear to be indefinite, but all visible and painful experiences have an appointed end, and it is comforting to know that we are not alone. *"For the Lord your God goes with you; he will never leave you nor forsake you"* (Deut. 31:6 NIV).

The story of the Kings' is an evidence that God continues to hear and answer the prayers of His people in His perfect time and according to His perfect will. *"The eyes of the Lord are on the righteous, and His ears are attentive to their cry* (Even when the process seems illimitable)*"* (Ps. 34:15 NIV).

We are encouraged to trust in the Lord wholeheartedly (Prov. 3:5), not in people. God alone knows and declares the end from the beginning (Isa. 46:10). Medical professionals have their place in helping with the knowledge that they obtained through studies, but the Word of the Lord still stands true and relevant today. *"He sent His word and healed them, And delivered them from their destructions"* (Ps. 107:20 NKJV). Karl's level of restoration thus far is not a result of man's intervention, but God's!

"For I know the plans I have for you," declares the Lord, *"plans to prosper you and not to harm you, plans to give you hope and a future"* (Jer. 29:11 NIV). Is this promise still relevant, even through difficult circumstances? It certainly is! God is integrous and cannot lie! Karl's future is still in front of him.

The History of How We Met

KARL RESIDED IN Florida and I in New York. We came in contact with each other in the summer of 2002 while he was visiting his family in New York.

After returning to his home state of Florida, we kept in touch. We developed a long distant relationship, which continued for two and a half years. This became somewhat unbearable. Therefore, we saw it fit to end it.

During our time of being apart, we dated individuals who were unworthy of even one moment of our time. In the midst of us dating other individuals, Karl and I continued conversing occasionally. Was this so because God has destined for us to be together?

In the year 2015, his mom became deathly ill and succumbed to her illness. After which, his grandmother also succumbed to her illness and passed away in that same year. It was as a result of such sad occasions that God saw it fit to divinely bring us back together.

We conversed daily, and we joyfully rekindled what I believe to be a seed sown that potentially sprouted as was predetermined by God. We fell deeper in love after making our relationship official in 2016. It was evident to both of us that we were created for each other, so marriage was spoken of frequently.

Unfortunately, at the end of 2016, Karl lost his job, became depressed, and at times, he felt hopeless. Having experienced such a devastating series of events made the job loss more difficult. Not having the comfort and moral support of his mother and grandmother was a difficult period in his life, especially as a young man who loved his independence.

Karl's joblessness continued throughout the year of 2017. "But God!" He was working things out for Karl's good, *"And we know that in all things God works for the good of those who love him, who have been called according to his purpose." (Romans 8:28 NIV)*. In the midst of the difficulties that Karl was experiencing, God allowed him to tap into the gifts that he entrusted to him. His involvement in church increased exponentially and so did his relationship with God. Absolutely nothing was wasted. God will ultimately use anything and everything for His plans and purposes to be manifested. His plans are always good, even when there is apparently nothing good to report.

Karl received a job-related breakthrough at the beginning of the year 2018 in Northwest Arkansas.

In January of the same year, Karl proposed to me.

Karl relocated to Arkansas in February, where he was faced with other unexpected difficulties due to the color of his skin. Racism was rampant. This was another hurdle that he had to overcome. However, by God's grace, this did not deter him from the purpose that was attached to this next God-predetermined venture in his life. He endured the racial conflicts, as he knew that God also had a plan in place.

Karl and I exchanged our vows as we made our covenant with God and ourselves official in October 2018.

With much excitement and great anticipation of a joy-filled marriage, we began our journey as a couple. We were two different people with differing personalities and sometimes, differing expectations. We had challenges, but we knew that our marriage was a covenant between God and us, so we were resolute to resolve every issue that we faced.

We had goals that were not farfetched, and two of them were to start our family and a ministry that would feed the less fortunate. We both had developed this God-given passion, and we were passionately looking forward to executing it.

A personal/sibling need arose that caused us to take a trip to Karl's home state of Florida in 2021, where he appeared to be ill and had to be taken to the emergency department at a near-by hospital.

You may face obstacles, but
never stop persevering.

The Traumatic Hospital Encounter

"And we know that in all things God works for the good of those who love him, who have been called according to his purpose."
Romans 8:28 NIV

IN FEBRUARY OF 2021, Karl woke up with a headache. Because of the intensity of it, he placed his hand on the back of his head. I then administered the prescribed blood pressure medication. There was no relief from the headache, so I did what I believed was the best thing to do and brought him to the hospital. He walked in unassisted and checked himself in. His blood pressure was checked, and the reading was an astounding 234/99, "but God!"

Karl was given additional blood pressure medication, intravenously, in an effort to regulate the pressure. This was without avail. This resulted in a CT scan being done after two hours of failed attempts to regulate his blood pressure.

Immediately, I called and requested prayer from our family members.

The CT scan results showed a hemorrhage (brain bleed). The helicopter service was summoned, and he was transported to another hospital where a neurologist was onsite. One can only imagine the fright and the anxiety that I would have experienced if it had not been for the grace of God and His incomprehensible peace with me while I was driving for thirty minutes while he was in flight.

At the time of arrival at the hospital, Karl was already being attended to by the nurses and doctors who, again, administered more medications. This time, however, the medications were for the stabilization of the brain bleed. He was then transferred to the ISCU unit for further observation and possible treatment. I was not allowed to remain with him because of the strict protocol that they had implemented.

The following day, February 8, 2021, with eagerness, I went to the hospital, and with Karl were the neurologist and the attendees checking the level of his alertness and physical abilities. They asked Karl if he knew who I was, among other questions, of which he answered them all correctly and without hesitation.

At this point, I received minimal information from the doctors concerning my husband, except that he had a brain bleed and that it was stabilized.

Karl expressed to me that he was a bit exhausted. The reason for the exhaustion was not unusual and was expected after a brain bleed. This was communicated to me by the doctors.

While I was with my husband, he spoke with a few family members, fed himself dinner, and brushed his teeth. After which, the physical therapist did a thorough evaluation/examination and concluded that there were no weaknesses in any of his limbs, as he followed all her instructions.

It was communicated to me that their plan was to keep him overnight for observation, which meant that he would have been discharged the following day.

The nurse that was on duty that same day told me that an MRI was to be scheduled, but she had no knowledge of the time. She asked the necessary questions, which, I suppose, were necessary for anyone who would have one done. All these questions were answered by Karl with minimum help from myself.

After visiting hours expired, I left my husband sleeping. At approximately seven p.m., I called the hospital to get information as to who his nurse would be for the night and to receive information regarding the MRI that they had supposedly scheduled. It was at that time that I was told that they were preparing him for the MRI.

After a few hours, I received an unexpected call from the nurse; it was a call that neither I nor anyone else was prepared to receive. She told me that my husband coded. I had no clue what that meant, but I knew it was not good. She then explained that he aspirated and lost oxygen to his brain. Without any time to process what I was hearing, I responded, "What did you do to my husband?"

I relayed this devastating information to his aunt and cousin, who we were staying with at the time of our visit to Florida.

In a state of shock and disbelief after what I heard and not knowing what I was going to see or hear on my arrival, I left for the hospital. With my eyes flooded with tears and me being disoriented and unfamiliar with the area, I had no idea what would have or could have happened. Nevertheless, I got there safely. Undoubtedly, the Lord was with me, and His angels have been given charge over me to keep me in all my ways (Ps. 91:11). During my transit to the hospital, my mom and the First Lady of the church I was a member of while living in New York were on a conference call with me, interceding to the only One we knew and knows that works miracles, signs, and wonders!

Before I entered the hospital, my mother told me firmly, "Do not be moved by what you will see or by what you will hear, but remember Who we serve." *"For we walk by faith, not by sight."* (2 Cor. 5:7 NKJV). On my arrival at the hospital, they were in the process of intubating him and inserting the central line.

It was incomprehensible, while all these things were unfolding, knowing that I left my husband quite fine and then hear that he had aspirated and coded. They had no explanation to present to me as to why all of this took place.

At this point, I was at a loss for words; "in shock" and "upset" are understatements.

In the wellness state (besides the already stabilized brain bleed) that I left my husband in, I returned to see him in such a condition. He was unresponsive and had tubes and attachments all over his listless body; it was puzzling. It was absolutely unbelievable!

What God has spoken through the apostle John should not be taken lightly because the enemy's desire still remains the same: to steal, to kill and to destroy (John 10:10a). *"Be sober, be vigilant; because your adversary the devil walks about like a roaring lion, seeking whom he may devour."* (1 Pet. 5:8 NKJV). It also stands true that Jesus has come, that we may have life, and have it more abundantly (John 10:10b). Was this evident? At that time, it did not seem evident.

Opposition may arise but continue to
finish the race.

The Nightmarish Days After

"Casting all your care upon Him,
for He cares for you."
(I Peter 5:7 NKJV)

AFTER LEAVING THE hospital, sleep and food were like my enemies; I desired neither. I was angry! After all, my husband should have been back home with me on the following day after the hospital visit. The next day, I felt as if I was held hostage and frozen in time. "What happened?" I asked. Who had the answers? Certainly not me or the doctors. No one but God had them!

Prayers became ceaseless! Some were short and some were long travails. Prayers became not only ceaseless, but they also became my daily bread, as were the healing Scriptures.

They were always at the forefront of my mind, and, from my heart, they proceeded from my mouth day after day. Family, friends, and I all prayed. 1 John 5:14 NIV states, *"This is the confidence we have in approaching God: that if we ask anything according to his will, he hears us."* Therefore, we did what the Scripture says, which is to, *"pray continually"* (1 Thess. 5:17 NIV).

I was encouraged not to be moved by what I see or hear, but walking into the ISCU and seeing my husband hooked up to all the machines was an indescribably difficult sight. I had to continue to trust that God would sustain him and restore him out of the sick bed. There were times that my tears had become my prayer language. I was lost for words and understandably in disbelief of all the series of events. Why did this happen? That was a frequent question I asked myself, with the hope that I would hear the answer, whether it was from myself or anyone, for that matter. God seemed silent, but during Job's ordeal, was He not silent also? God sometimes remains silent, and He always has a reason for doing so. I believe that we have to have faith and trust in God's silence.

Each day, I went to the hospital at the start of the visiting hours and stayed until the end of it. I was at my husband's side to give him as much support as possible. Although I needed moral support, he needed it more. The need for an advocate for my husband was an evident understatement, of which I had to become for him.

The nurse who worked on the day of the MRI had the same question that I had. She asked me, "What happened?" Then she said, "I left him fine."

When we (the family) tried to comprehend this complicated situation, the attending doctor's response was that she was not present. Therefore, it became even more puzzling, as the doctor who was expected to present some answers was, herself, clueless.

The puzzling days continued. I continued to be at his side daily, believing that God would keep him. Unsurprisingly, the doctor and other medical personnel were completely hopeless about his recovery. But I know in whom I believe in. I share the sentiment of the apostle Paul "…I believed; therefore I spoken…" (2 Corinthians NIV). Therefore, I continued to declare the promises of God whether I was present with him or not. For the Word of the Lord is Spirit and life. It is quick and it is powerful. It has all authority, as it is with its author. I continued to hold onto my faith in God so that my husband would pull through. The prayers continued.

After ten days, the decision was made to wean him off the ventilator. The tracheotomy and the percutaneous endoscopic gastrostomy (PEG) were emplaced.

The damage was done, and they wanted my husband out and out speedily. They had a very good reason for this.

Six days after the tracheotomy and PEG were emplaced, he was transferred to another facility who specialized in tracheotomy.

With all the hurt and the pain this hospital caused, I was relieved that he would no longer be held in their care or, maybe, better yet, their carelessness.

The situation may seem difficult,
"but God!"

The Tampa Fight and the Dream I Thought

> *"Those who sow with tears*
> *will reap with songs of joy."*
> Psalms 126:5 NIV

THE TRANSFER TO the facility where there were tracheotomy specialists was in Tampa. Although I was relieved that he was discharged from the hospital, the days ahead were extremely difficult because I was unable to be with him all day. This took the supernatural grace of God and patient endurance to bring me through. Visitation was limited to one hour each day for an extended period with only one visitor per day.

The facility was supposed to have been a rehabilitation facility as well, but my husband received very minimal therapy. This was untypical, considering his age.

After the tracheotomy was capped, I experienced some unforgettable moments, as my husband was able to say a few words. I grew more appreciative of seemingly minute blessings. I learned, through this process, that I should not take anything for granted. Karl had to be monitored while the tracheotomy was capped. Therefore, I did not always have the honor of hearing the voice of my husband during all my visits.

My expectations of this current facility were limited because of the lack of therapy sessions. This taught me more about humankind. As the Scripture exhorts, I do not put my trust in men, but in the Lord. He renewed my strength daily.

During Karl's stay, he was able to identify family members with the photos presented to him. This was not only encouraging, but also the highlight of some of my days because, with such a brain injury, this was considered to be a big deal.

After a week and a half of having the tracheotomy in place, Karl removed it himself. He was then transferred to a nearby hospital where he was admitted overnight to have it replaced. All of this was exhausting and traumatic, to say the least. After all that happened, who would want to entrust their loved in another hospital's/physician's care? But God gave me the peace of mind during the overnight stay.

After the replacement of the tracheotomy and the readmission to the facility, Karl was closely monitored to avoid the same occurrence.

At this same facility, the doctors were, for the most part, unreachable, which led to more frustration, as there were, again, more unanswered questions. I must say that there a few nurses who were not "pay-check" nurses. They had their patients' best interest at heart and gave as much information that was at their disposal. This gave me a little comfort and peace of mind.

I will be fair and give credit where credit is due. The speech therapist who was assigned to Karl was very understanding as well as willing and eager to work with him according to his needs. She recommended a barium swallow test, and the results of it would have determined whether or not he would be able to consume his foods by mouth. This test was futile at the time, but this did not diminish her high expectations for his recovery.

I was not moved by what I saw nor by what was communicated to me by any medical personnel. I remained constantly in prayer and did not allow my faith to be shaken.

Karl was at this facility for a month, and, in my estimation, my husband's progress declined. He was not getting the level of therapy that he needed and also being restraint. Me not knowing at the time that restraints, at any level, were not good for brain injured patients. His hands were consistently placed in restraints. This was a continuous practice by the medical personnel unless I was there to release him and give him some level of freedom. However, after some time, he remained in the restrained position, after which the brain readjusted to what it became accustomed to. Were they not aware of the negative effects that the restraints would have on his recovery? This was the method they chose. My guess is that it was the easy way out for the staff; this method alleviated the need to closely monitor him. They did this in an effort to alleviate the possibility of him removing the trach, as he did before, and getting out of the bed. He tried to do these things on a number of occasions.

The social worker's suggestion for Karl to be transferred to an acute care facility, where he would be able to get the therapy that was needed, was executed. The acute care facility was very highly rated. Their success rate was quite motivating. This was, at least, something to look forward to at this point because everything and everyone had failed to deliver what was promised. This expectation was topped with an ideal situation, as I was given the opportunity to be with him, in the same room, twenty-four seven. This would also mean that

I would be a couple of hours away from his aunt and cousin, having no one with us for physical or moral support.

As another chapter was getting ready to unfold, I packed up our car and headed three hours away from family. It was difficult because we were headed into the unknown. Would my expectations be met? How would I cope with the aloneness? What was waiting for us? With multiple questions, I kept my gaze on the only One who knows the past, the present, and the future, and He is ever faithful and trustworthy. The Lord our God has always been gracious to us.

> *"The Lord has done great things*
> *for us, and we are filled with joy."*
> Psalms 126:3 NIV

The transfer to the acute care rehab was accomplished. Besides their great ratings, they were known for their aggressive therapy regimen. This was definitely what my husband needed. Would my expectations for them to be

effective and efficient enough to help him get
back on his feet be met? I trusted the ratings,
but before long, I began to experience some
level of disappointment.

The excitement of being with him still
existed, but there was another hurdle awaiting
us as a result of the injury. There was a great
deal of spasticity and dystonia, which was
extremely painful for him. It was emotion-
ally debilitating to watch my husband experiencing such levels of pain, discomfort, and
sleeplessness. Looking back at all these experiences, I know undoubtedly that God has
been with us *"Be strong and courageous. Do not
be afraid or terrified because of them, for the Lord
your God goes with you; he will never leave you nor
forsake you." (Deuteronomy 31:6 NIV)*.

He was seen by several medical specialists
which included pulmonary, rehab, and internal
medicine specialists as well as a neurologist.
The physical, occupational and speech therapists were assigned to him, and he started
therapy immediately.

There were a few nurses that were very attentive and understanding, and so, my level of trust was raised a bit. One of those nurses mentioned that one of the physical therapists was well sought after. He was highly recommended because of his expertise and his diligence in working with patients. I expressed my desire to have him work with my husband, and I had to literally persist and insisted that he would work with him. My persistence paid off, and the interest that he showed in getting my husband up and about was even more than I expected. However, due to the dystonia and the spasticity, it was a challenge to get him up and standing. Nevertheless, he remained steadfast.

I learned of a medication that was able to alleviate the spasticity and the dystonia to an extent, and after much deliberation with the doctors, they finally agreed to prescribe it. They started him on the minimum recommended dose but refused to increase it to optimize its effect. This was a result of them not being appreciative of the assistance and recommendations that I was receiving from other doctors in New York.

There were times of verbal disagreements with the doctors, the nurses and I. I was graced by God to be present to advocate for my husband. It was a pleasure doing so. Otherwise, who would?

I had many sleepless nights. I cried many tears. Headaches were not a few, but in spite of it all, I continued to believe in God to give us a breakthrough. For He is the God of breakthroughs.

The doctors were not at all pleased with the fact that I was privileged to receive medical advice from the doctors in New York, so they decided that it was time for us to depart from their facility. They worked hard to have my husband discharged. At this point, the best thing to do was for us to travel to New York, where we would have the help and support of family and friends. To execute such a plan was no easy task, and it was costly because he could only travel for such a distance in a medical transport, which had to be paid out of pocket. I persevered, and God never ceased to intervene and amaze us. We have known Him as Jehovah Jireh, He Provides, (Gen. 22:14) and Jehovah Gibbor, the Man of War (Gen. 15:3). He fights for His children indeed. The battles belong to the Lord!

> *"This is what the Lord says to you:*
> *'Do not be afraid or discouraged*
> *because of this vast army. For the*
> *battle is not yours, but God's."*
> 2 Chronicles 20:15 NIV

Finally, he got to the facility in New York. That facility was a huge mistake. I began to question the decision that I made to move to New York. Could the situation get any worse? There were three nightmarish days. First, no visitors were allowed. Therefore, I was given the opportunity to FaceTime my husband instead. Secondly, it was obvious that he was not doing well. I made my observation known to the charge nurse. Thirdly, it was apparent that, from what I was able to observe via

FaceTime, his condition was oblivious to them, so they did nothing about it.

On May 31, 2021, I instructed them to have him transported to the hospital via an ambulance, which they did. On arrival at the hospital, as per usual, his vitals were checked, and lo and behold, his temperature was 104 degrees. I learned afterwards that this was something that should have been totally avoided. A temperature as high as his was a detriment to his recovery. "But God!" It was obvious that they were inefficient in carrying out their duties. How much more could he tolerate? Had he not gone through enough? Oh, how great the process had been, but I reiterate, God was present! In His greatness and sovereignty, He kept us!

While being admitted in the hospital, he received a series of tests. He remained hospitalized for two and a half weeks. Because he was in the hospital, he was no longer receiving the much needed therapy. Therefore, the recovery progress not only stopped, but he also experienced a great setback.

I could not get him out fast enough, but having the support of our family and friends made a huge difference. There was a great sense of ease. What a blessing they have been!

After the two and a half weeks stay in the hospital, Karl was transferred to a subacute care facility. This was now the fifth facility he has been in since the ordeal all began in Florida. I had to continue to stay strong in the Lord and in the power of His might (Eph. 6:16) and persevere with patient endurance. We know that our future is not held in the hands of the doctors or anyone else, but only in the hands of God!

God Kept Us!

The Battle Continued - But God!

"Have I not commanded you?
Be strong and courageous. Do
not be afraid; do not be discour-
aged, for the Lord your God will
be with you wherever you go."
Joshua 1:9 NIV

THERE IS NO other term that I could use to describe our experiences, but a continuum of war. Shortly after he was admitted to the fifth facility, a new battle arose. For four-teen days, I was unable to visit my husband because he had to be quarantined. But God had other plans!

There were a few proficient CNAs and nurses. These I refer to as "not-for-paycheck" employees. Those employees cared not only for the physical needs of the patients, but also for their emotional and psychological needs. May the others receive a touch of heart from the Lord, be delivered from the hardness of their heart, and receive a heart of compassion. Otherwise, their employment should be no place but the morgue where the deceased are temporarily housed and there are no emotional effects to ill treatment.

Karl had many sleepless nights, but God provided the people who cared enough to offer aid in my absence.

Again, the therapy services they offered were insufficient in getting him back on his feet. The times that were suggested by them were definitely not administered. At times, they did ten minutes of physical therapy per day. This was communicated to me by a family member of another patient in the adjoining room. After trying to have his scheduled therapy time changed, on several occasions in order to give me the opportunity to be present, it was all denied. So, they continued to do the minimal. May the Lord my God help the patients who have no one to advocate for them. From my experience, many of those facilities evidently lie in order to gain more patients for financial gain. Are peoples' lives all about making money? They accept patients and do very little to help them gain their independence or to get back to at least some level of normalcy. Is it that the longer the recovery, the longer they keep them and the more money obtain? The love of money is a root of all kinds of evil (1 Tim. 6:10).

There were days when Karl would express the ill treatment he received in our absence. Having received such information was concerning, but I have learned not to be anxious about anything. Through prayer and supplication with thanksgiving, I should let my requests be known unto God. In spite of it all, because the level of my trust in God had accelerated, and the Lord guarded my heart and mind with His peace which surpasses all understanding, I had no doubt that God would sustain him during his time of being processed for purpose.

At the end of August 2021, Karl was again transferred to another hospital because of what is called paroxysmal sympathetic hyperactivity, otherwise known as neurostorming. This bears the resemblance of a seizure, so it was mistaken as such. For a person with such a brain injury has he had obtained, a seizure could cause an alarm because of the detrimental effects that it could further cause.

Having him transferred to that particular hospital was adding to the nightmarish experiences that I would rather live without. They refused to discharge him, even when I signed him out. They held on to him as if he was a prisoner. After many hours passed, I was told that he had tested positive for COVID-19. He was admitted for a total of fourteen days. When I was given the opportunity to see him, he looked distressed. His speech was not as it was when I last saw him. Therefore, I had him stick out his tongue, and, to my amazement, he had the worst case of thrush that I have ever seen or heard of. This prevented him from swallowing, and his speech was greatly affected, as his tongue had become heavy and painful. If this was left untreated, it would have posed the risk of the infection spreading further into the body with serious consequences. Sadly, none of the medical personnel noticed it, which was an indication that his oral hygiene was ignored. Thank God for my ability to be vigilant and observant. It was after my observation that the nurses and the attending doctor became aware of this medical issue and began treatment. Whenever I was present, I presented myself as my husband's advocate, but the need also existed in my absence. This was quite concerning, but God, the omnipresent, omniscient, and omnipotent has always been and will always be Karl's Divine Advocate. He preserved him during his horrendous stay.

After he was discharged, he went back to the subacute rehabilitation facility where the battle continued. At the end of 2021, the therapist fractured his toe and refused to report it. Therefore, it was left unattended and untreated. The therapist was unaware of Karl's ability to communicate and articulate what had happened

to him while he was in his care, let alone shock-
ingly reveal his full name. Because of Karl's
quiet demeanor at the time (I believe that God
had it to be so), I had to further expose those
employees who were detrimental to physically
and sometimes mentally challenged patients.
The therapist thought he would have had a
well-kept, intentional secret. Unknowingly, the
level of Karl's cognitive skill restoration was
also a well-kept, unintentional secret. Not only
did I discover the discoloration and the fractured, smashed, swollen, and pained toe, but I
also had to make a request to have it examined.
After my initial request, it took another week
for an x-ray to be ordered and executed, which
confirmed the fractured toe. Even then, they
refrained from sharing this information with
me. It was one of the nurses who communicated this unfortunate information to me in the
form of a question, and with great astonishment,
he asked, "Didn't they tell you?" Of course
not! After all, the incident should have been
reported by the therapist and he did not, so they,
too, thought it fit to withhold this finding.

I confronted the supervising nurse regarding the finding, and, when she questioned Karl as it relates to the cause of the injury to his toe, to her surprise, he revealed to her and me the full name of the physical therapist. She was unaware of his full name and so was I, but Karl knew it. Nobody ever apologized for the incident. The only obvious confirmation of what the therapist did was that he was no longer allowed to work with Karl, and he avoided us at any cost. What a shame! But God will deal with them in His own time and in His own way. The promise still stands, *"Vengeance is Mine, I will repay, says the Lord"* (Rom. 12:19b).

This was undeniably irritating, and it aggravated every fiber of my being, to say the least, especially because it is a known fact that pain, in any form, should be avoided because of the impact that it has on a person with this kind of brain injury. Pain increases the levels of dystonia and painful spasms all over the body, which are excruciating and, for the most part, unbearable. He remained with a painful, swollen, discolored, undiagnosed fractured toe for over a week, being fed pain meds without having the knowledge of the root cause of the pain addressed.

After this finding was revealed to me, I received a call from a lab personnel who saw Karl for occasional lab work. The call was to inform me of an upcoming procedure called cardia catheterization or coronary angiogram. This procedure was ordered because of the discoloration of his toe. One would think that they would have told the lab technician of the cause for the discoloration. I had to break the news to her, to which she also responded in shock. The unnecessary, painful procedure was canceled.

After the many fights, I decided to take Karl home where he would be well taken care of. After he was discharged from the subacute facility, he was then placed into an outpatient facility where he received speech, physical, and occupational therapy.

The Divine Restoration

"But I will restore you to health and heal your wounds,' declares the Lord," Jeremiah 30:17a NIV

OUR GOD NEVER ceases to amaze us! His efficacious grace has been extended to us daily as we continue in our process for purpose. When we were physically and psychologically weak, His strength was manifested within us.

In January 2022 to June 2022, Karl was accepted to a prominent and very promising physical, occupational, and speech therapy facility. Oh, how disappointed we were in the quality of care. Patient care is not everyone's priority. How unfair their choice is to the patient and their family! The deception of these facilities was appalling, but not shocking, for it is written, "The love for money is the root of all kinds of evil..." (1 Timothy 6:10 NIV). This includes the evil of receiving payments for something that is not delivered. What a shame!

At this particular facility, our goal and expectations were to have Karl walking. This he did at home and not at any of the therapy sessions. After I shared this amazing milestone with the therapist, it was then he started to have Karl walk, but at a very minimal distance.

Karl's pace was more than what the physical therapist could provide for him. So, after a few sessions, they decided to discharge him with the lame excuse that the insurance will no longer cover the costs for any more sessions. I found out that this was a lie. Oh boy, these facilities' goals were always for the coins.

My expectation was not met as I expected, but God intervened, and we continued to put our trust in God and not in man. God never fails.

Before his discharge, I requested that an email be sent within the facility to ask if any of their therapists would be willing to do in-home therapy sessions. I stated that it would be paid out-of-pocket. To my surprise, my request was ignored. This shows the level of interest and care that these people have for those who are in need of their services and expertise. While they were planning his discharge, God was opening another door. Karl remained at home for a month without professional therapy before he was accepted to another facility, which came with high recommendations by a few medical teams.

In August of 2022 to March 2023, as the journey continued, Karl was again accepted to another facility. This one, I must say, had a different approach to patient care and their recovery. They were consistent in their efforts to help him become independent in his daily routine and return to normalcy. Their efforts were encouraging, and they taught me how to enhance what they were trying to accomplish. After a few therapy sessions, Karl began to walk at every session for approximately four hundred feet. What a God we serve!

The physical therapist never failed to help Karl in every way possible. Her care went beyond her paycheck. She helped us tremendously by getting equipment and assistance for home. God can use anyone He pleases and anyone who avail themselves to Him.

There is always a bad apple in every bunch, isn't there? There was one person from the personnel who did not like the challenge that she had to face some days when Karl experienced uncontrollable spasticity, so she decided that it was time to end his sessions. She did this abruptly. She uncompassionately discharged him without giving me the chance to find a replacement therapist. She also negatively influenced the other therapists and soon after, she also decided to discharge my husband. But God kept me encouraged! I know that He works strategically to accomplish His plans and purposes, so He continues to do what only He Himself can do! What a mighty God we serve!

In my efforts to speed up his restoration process, I also hired a personal trainer to help with the strengthening of his core and his muscles. This helped tremendously for a while, until the hirelings became familiar and too comfortable with us and began to slack off. What is wrong with people who decide to go into these professions? Are they in them only for personal gain or for a buck or two? What happened to giving themselves to passionate care?

After this extended period of dealing with an anoxic brain injury and what seemed impossible to the doctors and the therapists alike, God continued to show that He was strong and mighty on our behalf as He continued to restore Karl's nervous system back in divine alignment. What a mighty God we serve! With God, all things are possible!

"The righteous cry out, and the Lord hears them; he delivers them from all their troubles." Psalm 34:17 NIV

The Amazement of God

*"Praise be to the Lord God, the God
of Israel, who alone does marvelous
deeds. Praise be to his glorious
name forever; may the whole earth
be filled with his glory. Amen and
Amen."* Psalms 72:18-19 NIV

THE ROAD TO recovery for Karl still continues.
For the doctors and nurses to have seen him as
a hopeless case, I now can say my God answers
prayers and still performs miracles. He is a
God who sits on the throne and intervenes in
the affairs of His people. Our awesome God
works wonders and has demonstrated His
power among His people. (Ps. 77:14).

The tear-soaked pillows, the sleepless
nights, the heartaches, the headaches, the trust

that was lost in the medical systems, and the financial hardship had not taken God by surprise. He knows the end from the beginning. *"Your eyes saw my substance, being yet unformed. And in Your book they all were written, The days fashioned for me, When as yet there were none of them." (Ps. 139:16 NIV).* Despite all that we have been through, our faithful God and Father is a way maker, a Restorer, a Provider, a Miracle Worker, a Promise Keeper, a Comforter, a Healer, and a Friend.

The story of the Kings journey continues, and we will continue to trust in the Lord with all our hearts. We will not lean unto our own understanding, but in all our ways, we will acknowledge Him and He shall direct our path (Prov. 3:5-6). Our times and our lives are entrusted in His capable hands.

Karl's complete restoration is yet to be manifested, but we are confident that it will happen because our Redeemer lives. God does everything good (Gen. 1:12) and very good (Gen. 1:31).

The progress that Karl has made thus far cannot be accredited to doctors, therapists, or any other medical personnel. All the glory belongs to God. He is the God of all flesh; with Him, there are no impossibilities.

After he was an inpatient at the last facility for seven months, I felt the urge to take Karl home, and I followed my intuition. The day he came home was the very day that we began to see a greater level of progress, physically, cognitively, and otherwise. There were no more negative words spoken over his life, nor was there any more neglect to face in our absence. The atmosphere of faith, encouragement, prayer, praise, and worship were now constant.

While at home, Karl desired to begin walking again on his birthday. Our great God granted him the desire of his heart. He took a couple of steps, as my mom and I assisted him by hold each of his arms. What a day of rejoicing that was. We shed tears of joy as we celebrated and worshipped our indescribable, amazing God.

"Ask and it will be given to you; seek and you will find; knock and the door will be opened to you." (Matt. 7:7 NIV) God our Lord does not disappoint. His promises are in Him, amen!

After his birthday, standing and taking steps continued. We continue to see the awe-struck wonders of God daily, as his restoration continues. If we had not the faith of God or believed in the supernatural abilities of God, we would have been blown away.

And the best is yet to come!

> *"Then the Lord answered me and said: "Write the vision and make it plain on tablets, that he may run who reads it. For the vision is yet for an appointed time; But at the end it will speak, and it will not lie. Though it tarries, wait for it; because it will surely come, It will not tarry."* (Habakkuk 2:2-3 NKJV).

Conclusion

*"Heal me, Lord, and I will be
healed; save me and I will be saved,
for you are the One I praise."*
Jeremiah 17:14 NIV

THE ABOVE SCRIPTURE has been my husband's
personal cry to the Lord, and as promised, the
Lord has done just that. He has healed him;
He has saved him from the hands of the enemy.
How fitting it is that we continue to give our
great and indescribably awesome God and
Father the praise that is due to Him. We will
bless the Lord at all times, and His praises
shall continually be in our mouths. We do so
not only because of what He has done for us,
but also for who He is to us. Although there
were some days when I wished all the atrocities

would go away, I knew that everything would work together for our good because we do love the Lord, and, undoubtedly, we are called according to His divine purposes (Rom. 8:28).

It is always God's desire that His people have an intimate knowledge of Him. He gives each person the opportunity to do so, and He does so by using various methods.

It is, without doubt, that hearing God is not enough in knowing and experiencing Him intimately. One such methods or means in which God, in His infinite wisdom, allows is suffering. *"It is good for me that I have been afflicted, That I may learn Your statutes"* (Ps. 119:71 NKJV). By His divine wisdom, only what is sufficient to fulfill His plans and purposes will He allow.

Job heard of God by what was spoken of Him, but it was through his suffering that his spiritual eyes were opened to a greater dimension of the awestruck wonders of who God is (Job 42:5). What a privilege it is to suffer for the purposes of God to be manifested!

God is indeed integrous. Therefore, it is impossible for Him to lie. His promises must be manifested because of their infallibility. It is with great confidence that I can declare that *BUT GOD 2* is coming soon, revealing the completion of Karl's divine restoration!

> *"My brethren, count it all joy when you fall into various trials, knowing that the testing of your faith produces patience."* *(James 1:2-3 NKJV)*

Acknowledgment

I WANT TO specially thank our family and friends, who have been there for us through the very difficult process and experiences we have had. We certainly could not have done it without your help and moral support.

May this book be a blessing to everyone. As you read, may you receive revelations of God, for He is love, omnipotent (all-powerful), almighty, faithful, forgiving, a provider, loving, a protector, a healer, a deliverer, a sustainer, and indeed, our miracle worker!

But GOD!
Finish The Race Strong

Printed in the USA
CPSIA information can be obtained
at www.ICGtesting.com
LVHW051024271023
762259LV00012B/205

9 781662 885204